365
Positive Words for
a Teenage Girl

Rebecca Dorothy Valastro

Copyright © 2011 Rebecca Dorothy Valastro

All rights reserved.
ISBN: 0-9954253-0-2
ISBN-13: 978-0-9954253-0-9
Published 2017.

All rights reserved. No part of this book may be reproduced by any mechanical, photographic, or electronic process, or in the form of a phonographic recording; nor may it be stored in a retrieval system, transmitted, or otherwise be copied for public or private use-other than for "fair use" as brief quotations embodied in articles and reviews-without prior written permission of the publisher.

The author of this book does not dispense medical advice or prescribe the use of any technique as a form of treatment for physical, emotional, or medical problems without the advice of a physician, either directly or indirectly. The intent of the author is only to offer information of a general nature to help you in your quest for emotional and spiritual well-being. In the event you use any of the information in this book for yourself, which is your constitutional right, the author and the publisher assume no responsibility for your actions.

I'm so happy I get to share this with you!

When I was in my first year of high school, we were all given an envelope with our name on it. We then wrote something nice, a "warm fuzzy" about each girl in the class and placed it in their envelope. The first time I read the contents of my envelope I felt so good inside, it brought a much-needed smile to my face. I began to read my envelope every day and soon I stopped concentrating on all the things I didn't like about myself and focused on all the good things that others had seen in me. 365, is essentially 365 warm fuzzies from me to you. You don't have to wait any longer to be amazing; you will soon learn that you already are :-)

      -Be the girl you were born to be-

          B xoxo

I AM AS BRIGHT & BEAUTIFUL
AS A SINGLE FLOWER

WHAT I LIKE ABOUT ME

Write on a piece of paper 3 things that you like about yourself. It can be that you have nice hair, that you are good at sport or even that you have nice handwriting. Whatever you like about yourself, write it down.

Now every morning when you get up, read those 3 things to yourself and remind yourself of how great you really are.

I know it feels strange and seems kind of weird, but why not give it a go? When I feel sad and don't want to face the day, I read my list and I feel better. Sometimes it even makes me smile.

AND you don't have to stop there, you can write 10 things you like about yourself. You can write as many as you like. The best part is, on a good day when you already feel great, it makes you feel even better!

I AM AS PRETTY AS A WHOLE FIELD OF FLOWERS!

I know it feels weird when you start to say things like, "*I am pretty*" -especially when you are not used to saying them. How many times have you said to yourself, I am pretty? Let me tell you, YOU ARE BEAUTIFUL. Feels funny hearing that doesn't it! But it's true... and the more you say it to yourself, the less funny it will feel and the more you will believe it, because YOU ARE absolutely 100% BEAUTIFUL.

**LIFE IS BRIGHT
AND SO AM I**

I'M PRETTY

FANTASTIC TOO

I AM A STARRRRRRRRRRRR

I SHINE BRIGHT

When you know you have to get something done or there is something that you want to do or achieve, but you always find an excuse for why you don't do it and a reason for why it isn't happening; I call SPRUNG! It's fear that is stopping you. Fear of not getting it right, fear of looking silly, fear of being laughed at and even fear of getting hurt. By allowing the fear to stop you, you are hurting yourself anyway. Never taking a step toward what you truly want, can stop you from feeling happy. The good news is, you can change that right now. You can take a step forward, sign up for the team, audition for the play, write a story or even tell that person how you feel. Every time you take a step, it will bring you closer to what you want. Have the courage to take one step.. Maybe it doesn't work this time but it's the many steps we take, that get us to the top.

I CAN MAKE IT UP ANY ROCKY STAIR

Sometimes I feel like I am going round and round in circles... that's ok I'm learning with each step I take ☺

**THERE IS NO
WRONG WAY**

**YOU CHOOSE
WHAT IS BEST
FOR YOU**

I AM CALM

I choose to remain calm when everything else gets a little crazy. With a couple of deep breaths, I can handle any situation calmly.

I AM FREE

I am free to choose who I want to be. If I sit
quietly and ask myself what it is that I want,
I will hear the answer come from within.
It will feel right to me.

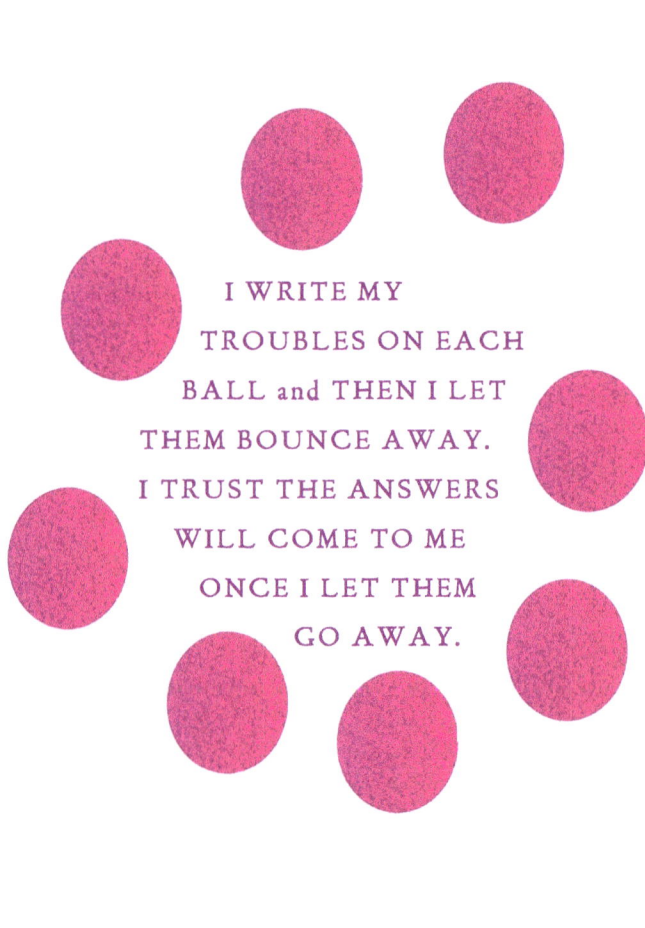

YOGA

I TAKE GOOD CARE OF MY BODY

Fashion Factory

I CREATE MY OWN FASHION & I LOOK GREAT

I KNOW WHAT IS BEST FOR

MY BODY - I LISTEN TO

MY INNER VOICE

I RESPECT MY BODY

I Like What

I See

in ME

I truly am Extraordinary

**I AM
INTELLIGENT**

**I TRULY AM
A WONDERFUL
FRIEND**

I CAN BE FRIENDS WITH EVERYONE

Where in the world would you like to go? It can be in Australia or a remote island. You get to choose anywhere you like. Have you picked it? Now say to yourself, *one day I am going to go there*. Cut out a picture or draw your place and put it on your wall. And guess what! You don't have to wait to visit there... pick something about your place and live it! If it's Paris, eat a croissant, if it's New York, have a slice of cheese pizza, if it's Hollywood, walk around with a pair of dark sunglasses on and pretend you are a Hollywood Star! Pick anything you like. Maybe lie on a towel for your tropical island or listen to some Egyptian music while drawing a pyramid. Escape to your place of travel and enjoy being there for a little bit... even if it's just pretend.

What do you love most in the world? Is it your pet, the sunshine, dancing, drawing, singing or listening to music? Is there a particular person you love or is it eating ice cream? I love warm days and warm soup when it's cold outside. I love to dance and sing out loud. I love to eat extra large popcorn at the movies and I love being with my family and friends. I love to shop and I love all kinds of shoes. I especially love Paris and I am so grateful to have travelled there. When I am having a bad day and feeling low, I think about all the things I love. The bad days don't seem so bad when I think about the things I am grateful for. When I focus on what is good in my life, I feel better. Maybe you could try it and see if it makes you feel good too.

THERE IS MORE THAN JUST ONE OPTION AND IT IS I THAT CHOOSES WHICH WAY I GO

AT ANY TIME I CAN CHANGE DIRECTIONS. I CHOOSE. IT IS NEVER TOO LATE NOR IMPOSSIBLE TO DO. I TRUST MYSELF TO KNOW WHICH DIRECTION TO TAKE.

When I feel myself panicking, I sit and take a deep breath in. Everything is going to be OK. Even if I can't see it and even if it hurts real bad, I am going to keep breathing and I am going to be OK.

When I breathe deeply I feel calm.

Take 3 long slow deep

breaths in and out.

With each new sunrise, start the day fresh.
You are renewed and can be whatever
it is that you want to be.

As the sun goes down, let go of what the day has been, for tomorrow is a new day with every opportunity for new things.

Sometimes it's hard to know

WHICH
WAY
TO
GO

BUT I
ALWAYS
FIND MY
WAY

Eventually!

PERSISTENCE

PERSISTENCE

PERSISTENCE

You CAN DO IT!

With persistence you can achieve. Make a plan today & keep going until you get there.

I Trust in Tomorrow

A New Day

is A New Beginning

There is always Light.
All I have to do is Open
my Eyes and look around.
It may be in a place I
least expect, but there
is always Help when
I Need it.

I AM NEVER ALONE...

I always have ME

The bestest friend I could ever have is me

That is why it is so important to take care of me first.

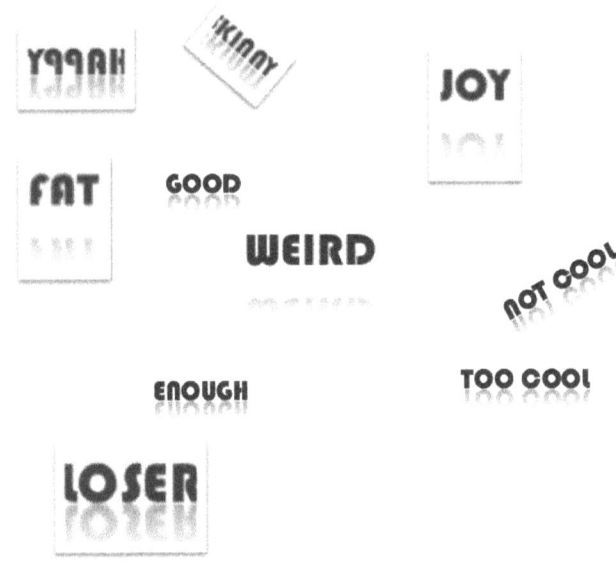

WORDS ARE ONLY WORDS UNTIL YOU PUT MEANING BEHIND THEM. For instance, Weird means Unique to me and is totally cool! Calling me a loser means you have poor judgment and you don't deserve my friendship. Sometimes, if someone calls me an idiot, instead I choose to hear, "you are soooooo intelligent!"

When people start using cruel words towards me, instead of feeling hurt I ask myself, how do I know exactly what they are thinking? Does it mean the same to me as it does to them? And if it's something quite full on like:

YOU ARE A FAT LOSER

Then I choose to drop a few letters of each word like a Y and an E and a T and an L. All of a sudden the words mean nothing at all:

OU AR A FA OSER

Makes no sense at all! The words are not complete because I don't allow them to be completed.

If someone calls you a nasty word or starts to pick on you, let a few letters drop, let the words drop. They really don't mean anything, because you are beautiful and perfect exactly as you are. You choose the meaning behind the words. If the words don't feel good, then I give them zero meaning.

I AM STRONG

YOU ARE GROWING STRONGER

AND STRONGER EVERY DAY

I RESPECT OTHER PEOPLE'S BOUNDARIES

NO ENTRY

I listen when people ask me not to do something that hurts them

Strength within creates bravery. As you grow stronger with each day, you become more brave, more open, more honest, more strong within yourself.

Believe in your most Sacred Dreams.

Break through the fear.

I Trust Myself.
I Trust that I Know What Next to Do.

I can choose to see the uniqueness in other people and see that it's just as beautiful as the uniqueness in me.

We all have something special to offer, whether it's being good at basketball, writing a story or making someone smile. We are all special in our own unique way.

Do something today that makes you feel happy.

Do you know how special you are?

If You Can Dream it..
You Can Make
It Happen.

Dream Something
　Awesome for Yourself!

With Planning Belief and Action

You Can Achieve Anything

I LIKE WHO I AM

I Deserve for
ALL my Dreams
to come True!

As I Grow I become more Wise & more Beautiful

I Choose to do my Best
to be Kind to Everyone

All girls are special and gorgeous and deserve to be looked after. You deserve to always be treated kindly and loved. You are special and gorgeous too.

Sometimes when we are feeling bad, we lash out at other people. When we are hurting, we sometimes hurt others. It's OK, you are not alone. We all have done it. The best thing we can do, is recognize when we are hurting someone else and stop. All girls are special and deserve to be treated with kindness. Let your beautiful heart shine, sparkling from within, as you start the new craze; the kindness within.

You do not have to accept when people treat you bad.

YOU ARE WORTHY OF HAVING GOOD FRIENDS.

I treat people with kindness and respect.

I AM A GOOD FRIEND.

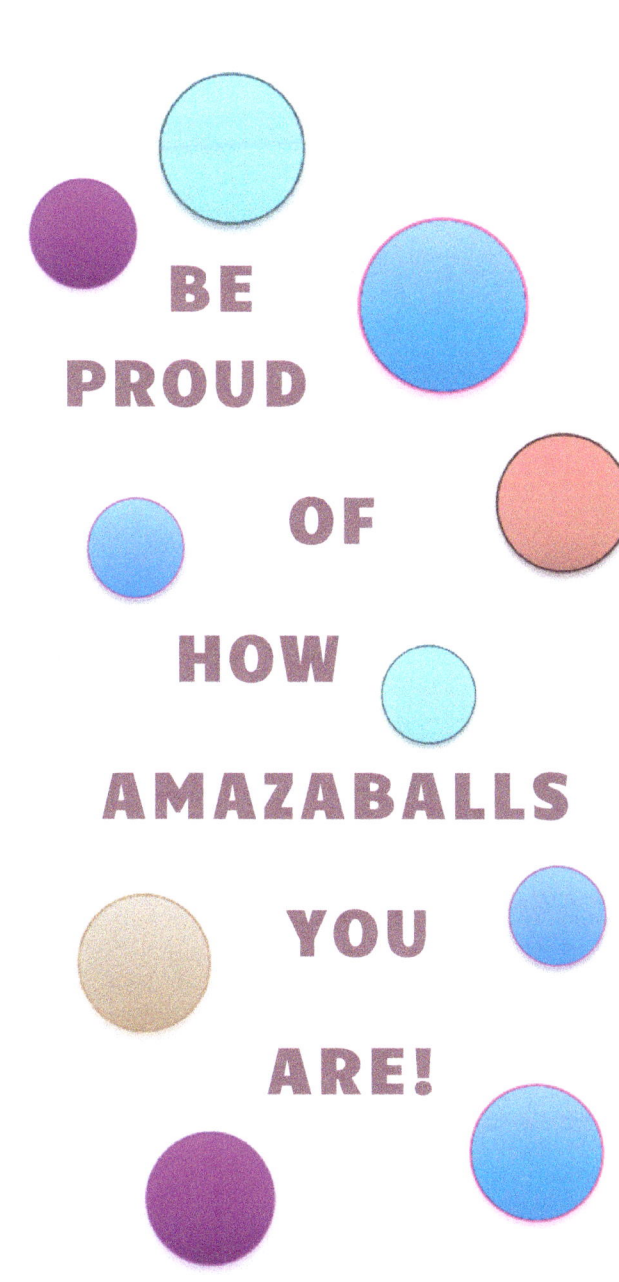

You are Bright, Beautiful and
Wonderful. You can be anything
you choose to be.

I create JOY in my world.
People feel good when
they are around me.

YOUR EYES ARE BRIGHT & BEAUTIFUL
YOUR EYES ARE BRIGHT & BEAUTIFUL
YOUR EYES ARE BRIGHT & BEAUTIFUL
YOUR EYES ARE BRIGHT & BEAUTIFUL
YOUR EYES ARE BRIGHT & BEAUTIFUL
YOUR EYES ARE BRIGHT & BEAUTIFUL
YOUR EYES ARE BRIGHT & BEAUTIFUL

**I SEE THE BEAUTY
IN YOU
I SEE THE BEAUTY
IN YOU
I SEE THE BEAUTY
IN YOU
I SEE THE BEAUTY
IN YOU
I SEE THE BEAUTY
IN YOU
I SEE THE BEAUTY
IN YOU
I SEE THE BEAUTY
IN YOU**

I hope you realize how special you are, how important you are, just as you are. If you ever feel like putting yourself down or you catch yourself saying something mean about yourself, I want you to HALT it as soon as you realize you are doing it and replace it with...

I AM A SPECIAL GIRL

YOU ARE A SPECIAL GIRL

I REMAIN ALERT
I PAY CLOSE ATTENTION
I TAKE IN ALL DETAILS
-WHICH HELPS ME TO MAKE
CONSCIOUS DECISIONS
THAT ARE RIGHT
FOR ME

IF YOU FEEL PRESSURED
YOU CAN ANSWER WITH
"LET ME GET BACK TO YOU"
THEN YOU CAN GO AWAY
AND DECIDE ON YOUR OWN
WHAT THE BEST ACTION
IS FOR YOU TO TAKE

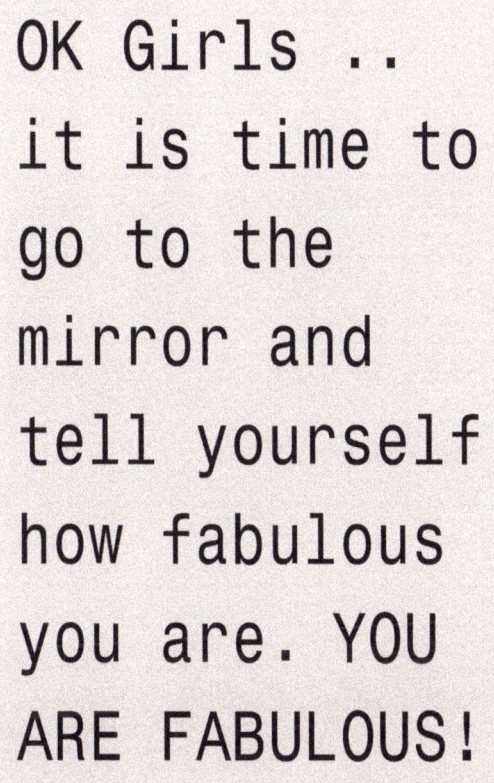

OK Girls .. it is time to go to the mirror and tell yourself how fabulous you are. YOU ARE FABULOUS!

Laughter is fine and expected :-)

SOMETIMES IT'S HARD TO SEE
THROUGH THE TREES BUT
WITH TIME EVERYTHING
BECOMES CLEARER

EACH MOMENT WILL PASS & NEW
HOPE WILL EMERGE

> AS WILL YOU
> STRONGER
> RESILIENT
> A BRAVE
> WARRIOR

SOMETIMES YOU FEEL THE NEED TO BE
ON YOUR OWN OR SIT ON YOUR OWN

TO GET SOME TIME ALONE

JUST FOR YOU

AND THAT IS OK

I CAN MAKE IT OVER ANY BUMP THAT MAY APPEAR ALONG MY ROAD

Life can be challenging and I AM CAPABLE of dealing with what may happen when it happens. I TRUST MYSELF to know what to do when it does happen and in the meantime I will not worry myself until it does or does not happen.

Make-up is at its best when it is kept light and barely there. You have such a beautiful face naturally, make sure we can still see it.

I NO LONGER COMPARE MYSELF TO OTHERS
I AM MAGNIFICENT

MY BODY IS PERFECT FOR ME
I AM KIND TO MYSELF
I LOVE ME

Not everyone will like you and that is OK. I know it seems really important right now, but in 6 years time when you are working, in college or even travelling the world, this day won't seem so bad. Let the ones who are mean be the jerks, you have better things to do, like plan your future surrounded by wonderful people, living all your dreams till the very end.

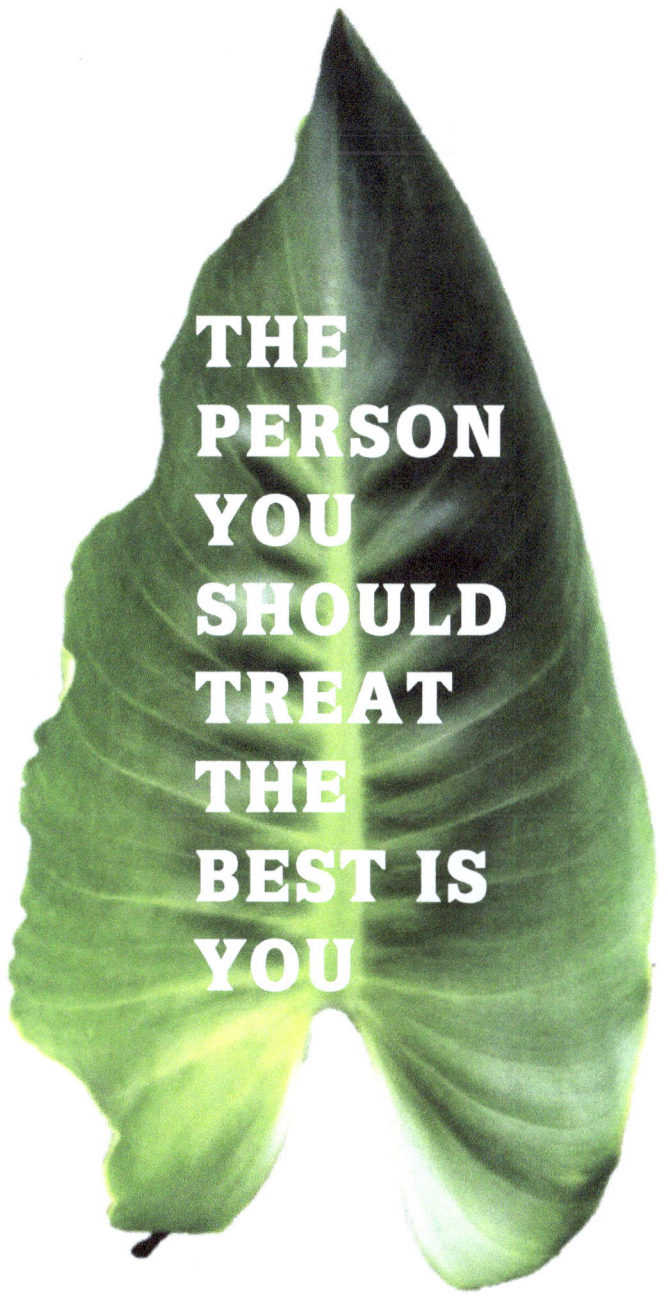

When first performing a task, it can be difficult. With practice it gets easier.

THE MORE I PRACTICE
THE EASIER IT BECOMES

BE PROUD OF YOU!
YOU ARE DOING
AN AMAZING JOB!

When I am having a bad day
I say, "that's ok" for I know tomorrow
will come and I will feel better.

The Sun is Shining and So AM I

There is no one else in the world exactly like you. That makes you pretty Unique & Special too.

There is one YOU and YOU have a very important job to do Being YOU.

İ LİSTEN TO OTHERS AND LET THEM HAVE THEİR SAY WİTHOUT İNTERRUPTİNG
İ know how good it feels when someone listens to me

WHEN YOU HAVE A GOAL İN MİND STAY FOCUSED
Sometimes we are easily distracted just as we are about to reach our goal

Persistence
Planning
Belief

- with this I CAN Achieve!

SHOOT FOR THE STARS

No Dream is too Big when you take it One Step at a Time

YOU ARE
NATURALLY
CREATIVE

*It is natural for me
to create, because
all I have to do
is imagine...*

Pick one thing you are grateful for, then say out loud...

" THANK YOU "

It can be for your best friend or a piece of chocolate cake, even a glass of cold water on a hot day! You get to choose.

Thank you for

    Everything

        You do!

           Your

      Kindness

Does not go

Unnoticed

Don't be in too much of a hurry to grow up. Some of the most fun things in life are as simple as sliding down a slide, eating a melting ice-cream and chasing each other through the park. There are so many things that we rush, growing is one we should take slowly... after all, the younger you are, the more you get away with!

LAUGH OUT LOUD!

Do it in the mirror and see how silly you feel!

Guaranteed you'll LAUGH some MORE!

WHAT CHANGES THE WORLD
IS HOW PEOPLE FEEL.

CAN YOU MAKE SOMEONE SMILE TODAY?

I AM HAPPY AND FULL OF LIFE!

Sometimes we have to fake it till we make it. Practice being happy today.

YOU CAN REINVENT YOURSELF TODAY

Be whoever you want to Be.

With every rising day, you can choose to be different.

You can choose to be anything you want!

BREATHE DEEPLY
DRAW IN FRESH AIR

ENERGIZE

Positive thoughts will fill you with ENERGY

Try thinking of 3 great things TODAY

I know the answers that are right for me. I listen to that feeling inside.

I take good care of myself

EVERY DAY

I AM WORTH LISTENING TO

**I KNOW THE RIGHT TIME
TO LISTEN
AND
THE RIGHT TIME
TO SPEAK**

**YOU ARE RESPONSIBLE
FOR YOUR FUTURE
IT IS OK
FOR YOU TO
CONCENTRATE
ON YOU**

I AM RESPONSIBLE FOR ME

Take Good Care of YOU Today

The Greatest Love you will Feel

Will come from  **YOU**

wE are All ImPortAnt

I chOOse To SuPPort MYself & thOsE arOUnd ME.

Sometimes when people get angry,
it is because of many things.
Sometimes it all builds up inside.
And even though it can be difficult,
it's better for everybody when we
respond with kindness. Makes us all
feel a little bit better inside.

When you see someone angry or upset -try giving them a smile. Sometimes the smallest things can make us feel better, especially when someone shows us a smile.

There is no one else just like You

You Are Amazing

I AM NICE AND LOVING TO EVERYONE

**PEOPLE FEEL GOOD
WHEN THEY ARE
AROUND ME**

THE WORLD İS İMPORTANT

İ TAKE CARE OF MY ENVİRONMENT

İ AM İMPORTANT

İ TAKE CARE OF ME

**TIME IS ON YOUR SIDE
USE IT TO ACHIEVE
ALL YOUR DREAMS**

We ALL do silly things and some of the things we do, we are not proud of. Sometimes the silly things we do make us feel so awful inside, that we wish the world would swallow us up and hide us away. Hang in there my friend... with time you will feel better. You will think about it less and less, until one day, it is a distant memory. How could that possibly be? Time changes everything. I know it's hard to believe, especially if it happened just yesterday, but as time goes by, bit by bit, day by day, you will feel a little bit better, until one day it becomes a memory that can no longer hurt you. Make a journal and note the days. I challenge you to see if you feel even the tiniest bit better in 1 month, 6 months, 1 year. Do you even think about it after 5 years?

It's OK for me to feel angry and upset; it's normal. If the bad feelings don't go away, it's OK for me to talk to someone - no problem is too small to ask for help.

This moment will pass, as do all moments. One day you will wake up and you will be living the dreams you set for yourself. So make plans, take action and watch them come to life.

If I saw you now, I would give you a hug. A hug is the best medicine anyone can buy. It makes you feel warm and safe inside, it allows you to wallow, scream and cry. And a hug does not necessarily have to come from another person. The most hugs I have had, has been from Teddy. Yep that's right my Teddy Bear. You are never too old nor too young, it's the perfect friend ready to hug. Teddy (my teddy bear) has certainly soaked up some tears. He was there for me when I thought no one else cared, he was there for me when I was too embarrassed and didn't want to share. He was there through the hurt and the pain, as my constant hug and confidant. Now a Teddy may not be for everyone, but hugs come in all sorts of shapes and sizes, like a mum or a sister and even your best friend. But if you ever need to talk to someone who doesn't talk back ... well then Teddy will always be your friend.

Is there someone you know who looks kind of sad? Could you ask them if they are OK? Sometimes the show that somebody cares, can make us all feel a little bit better inside.

IT'S OK TO FEEL BLUE

we all do sometimes

TODAY IS A NEW DAY

full of new possibilities

LEAN ON YOUR FRIENDS

IF YOU DON'T FEEL SAFE TO TALK TO FRIENDS

(A SCHOOL GUIDANCE COUNSELOR CAN HELP)

IF IT ALL FEELS JUST TOO DIFFICULT

PLEASE CALL A HELP LINE

ANYTIME DAY OR NIGHT

PEOPLE CARE FOR YOU & WANT YOU TO BE SAFE

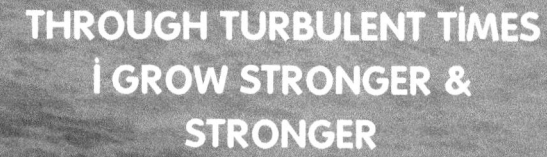

THROUGH TURBULENT TİMES
İ GROW STRONGER &
STRONGER

Is there a problem weighing you down or maybe keeping you awake at night?

Write it down on a piece of paper (even a paper bag will do), then write the outcome you would like to happen. Fold this piece of paper into the smallest square that you can manage and put it in a box, a tin or you can even rip it up and put it in the bin.

Know that your problem is now with your angels. No need to worry about this anymore, the right outcome for you has been set in motion and if there is some action you can take, devise a plan when you wake.

I HAVE CONFIDENCE IN MY ABILITY TO SOLVE MY PROBLEMS.

I CAN DO IT!

AMO LA VITA!
I LOVE LIFE

io fido in me

I TRUST IN ME

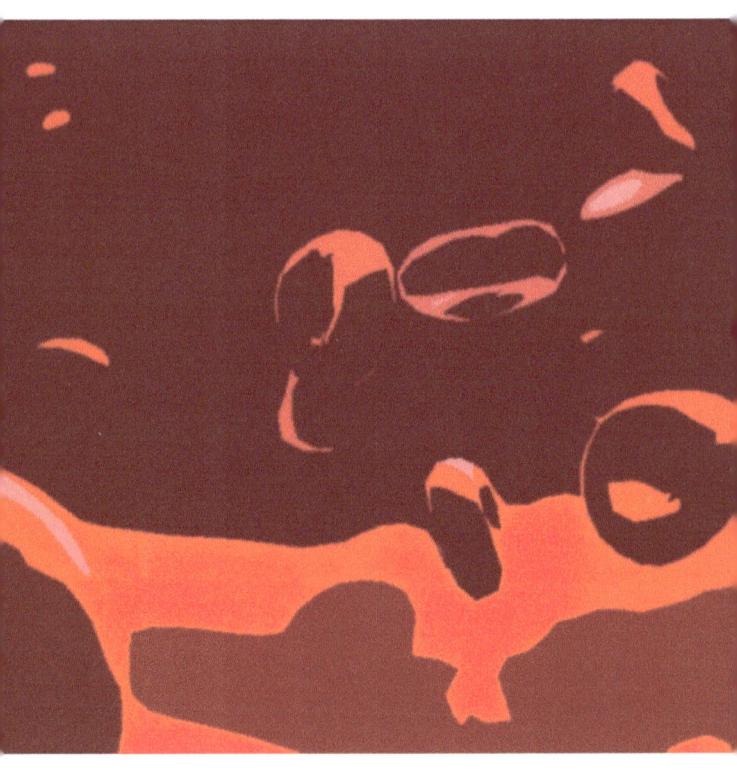

My body is producing millions of new cells every second of every day. I am renewed in each moment.

 EVERY DAY

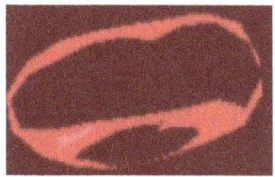 IS A NEW DAY

 I GET TO REINVENT

 MYSELF

i CHOOSE how i want to SHiNE

i find JOY in the things i CHOOSE TO DO

i SPARKLE

No one shadows me

*There is enough room for us
　　　　　All to SHINE*

Sometimes we need to be Willing to SEE it from another point of view.

You never know what you might SEE.

There is no wrong way. It's about the choices you make. If you find yourself going in a direction that doesn't seem right to you, then make the choice to change directions.

I trust myself to know when to change directions, when to leave a bad friendship or bad relationship, when to study, when to work, when to play and when to take time out for myself.

I SEE HOW WONDERFUL I AM
I CONTINUE TO ALLOW MYSELF TO BE FABULOUS!

THERE IS NO BETTER ME THAN ME! XOXO

SOMETIMES WHEN
I DON'T FEEL SO
GOOD AND I SMILE
-IT ENDS UP MAKING
ME FEEL GOOD
WHEN I SMILE AT
SOMEONE ELSE

GO TO A MIRROR
LOOK AT YOURSELF
GIVE A BIG CHEESY
GRIN & REPEAT
"I HAVE A
BEAUTIFUL SMILE"

It's not OK for people to swear at you. You do not have to take it, listen to it, nor accept it. You deserve to be spoken to with respect and kindness.

I SPEAK TO PEOPLE THE SAME
AS I WANT TO BE SPOKEN TO.
WE ALL DESERVE TO BE SPOKEN
TO WITH KINDNESS & RESPECT.

I WANT YOU TO HOLD YOUR HEAD HIGH TODAY

BECAUSE YOU HAVE A BEAUTIFUL FACE & A BEAUTIFUL SMILE BEAUTIFUL HAIR WITH AMAZING STYLE

WALK TALL AND PROUD
BECAUSE YOU ARE
AMAZING

I AM WHO I AM THANK GOD I AM!

I AM THE BEST ME THERE IS!

Think about something that deserves your attention. Anyone that treats you like crap does not deserve your attention. Change your attention to the things you do want, the people that are kind to you and the amazing future you have dreamed up for yourself.

You do not have to stay in a relationship if it is destroying your soul. If you feel sad more than you feel good, then something is wrong. You decide what's best for you because you are worth every desire that you can imagine for yourself.

Treat others how you want to be treated. Focus on being the best you that you can be. Awesome people will follow you through life, because you are amazing being the girl that you were born to be.

GOOD FRIENDS ARE IMPORTANT

THEY WILL BE WITH YOU FOR LIFE. THEY WILL NEVER JUDGE YOU OR MAKE YOU FEEL BAD FOR BEING YOU. THEY WILL ALWAYS BE THERE TO SUPPORT YOU, EVEN THOUGH THEY MAY NOT AGREE, THEY WILL STILL LOVE YOU.

I AM A GOOD FRIEND. I AM LOVING AND SUPPORTIVE. I VOICE MY OPINION AND ACCEPT THAT MY FRIENDS MAY NOT SEE IT THE SAME WAY AS I DO. I ACCEPT OUR DIFFERENCES AND I LOVE THEM ANYWAY.

I am worthy to receive all that is wonderful, positive, beautiful & great.

I am understanding and compassionate toward others.

I DO MY BEST EVERY DAY & I AM REALLY PROUD OF ME

I NO LONGER DOUBT MYSELF -I KNOW I CAN ACHIEVE ANYTHING

People will talk of mother love and sometimes we will struggle to understand. Perhaps we aren't getting along with our mother and some of us don't have a mother at all. Know this; Motherly Love can come in many forms, from an aunt, a teacher or a friend, even a father can be motherly too. Treasure what you do have, whatever form it comes in and know that one-day, you'll give some motherly love to someone too.

I AM LOVEABLE

I am loving & giving
I am truthful & honest
I am kind & caring
I am wonderful
I am amazing
I am Me

Look in the mirror & say to yourself

I am Loving & Giving
I am Truthful & Honest
I am Kind & Caring
I am Wonderful
I am Amazing
I am ME

It feels silly doesn't it...
but it sure does feel good too!

I Choose to do My Best at being Kind to Everyone

We ALL have our off-days and sometimes we snap at other people. I am not perfectly nice ALL the time, but I do try my best to treat others with kindness. Sometimes it's tough, but I do try my best.

Families come in all shapes and sizes. Some are blood related and some are your best friends. Family is those who support you, those who love you, those who will be there for you when you need them most.

i am surrounded by people who love me

I know when I should Apologize and I have the Courage to do so

You are a strong girl
You are incredibly
kind within

WHAT DO YOU WANT?

Do you want to be able to run 3km? Shoot a basketball from the 3-point line? Perhaps you want to learn to dance? Talk in front of the class, audition for the school play or buy a new pair of jeans? Perhaps you want to be a Hollywood Star or even the next Prime Minister! Whatever it is begin by making a plan. A step-by-step process of how you will get there. You can make your dreams a reality. Through planning and action you can achieve whatever you want.

I have a vision board. A collage of people and places I like. It also has my dream career and the things I strive to achieve. I stuck this up on my wall and every morning when I wake, it inspires me and reminds me of what I am striving for.

**YOU CAN DO IT!
I KNOW YOU CAN
I BELIEVE IN YOU**

Now go to the mirror and repeat

I CAN DO IT!
I KNOW I CAN
I BELIEVE IN ME

It is OK to feel a little scared and uncertain about what tomorrow brings. Believe in your own strength and ability to get through it. You are more amazing than you think.

I AM
RESILIENT & STRONG

What would you do, if you knew you couldn't fail? That whatever it was, you would be successful at it?

Think about it...

Have you got it in your mind?

OK... Now Do It!

What is it that's holding you back? If it doesn't work the first time, we can always give it another go. There are many ways to solve a problem as well as achieve our goals.

 I RELEASE FEAR

I AM CONFIDENT IN ME

I will not compromise my dreams. They are mine to create and mine to achieve.

ANYTHING IS POSSIBLE

I CAN DO IT!

When that negative thought comes creeping into your mind and you start saying mean things about yourself

HALT IT

Repeat after me:

I AM A BEAUTIFUL GIRL
I HAVE A KIND HEART
I AM PERFECT JUST AS I AM

When that negative thought comes creeping into your mind and you start saying mean things about someone else

HALT IT

Find something good about them:

- IS GOOD AT SPORT
- HAS A NICE SMILE
- MAKES PEOPLE LAUGH

I LET OTHERS DECIDE WHAT IS RIGHT FOR THEM. THEY HAVE THE RIGHT TO CHOOSE THEIR OWN DESTINY – JUST AS I CHOOSE MINE.

IF YOU ARE ANGRY WITH SOMEONE – CHOOSE SOMETHING NICE ABOUT THEM – JUST ONE SMALL THING AND SAY IT OUT LOUD. DO YOU FEEL ANY BETTER? TRY IT AGAIN

WHEN I GET ANGRY, I GO AND SIT ON MY OWN AND LET MYSELF CALM DOWN. I CAN THEN THINK MORE CLEARLY ABOUT WHAT IT IS I AM ANGRY ABOUT AND WHAT WOULD BE THE BEST OUTCOME.

IF YOU START TO FEEL YOUR BLOOD BOIL AS THE ANGER CREEPS UP INSIDE, TAKE A DEEP BREATH IN AND COUNT TO SIX BEFORE MAKING A COMMENT. OUR WORDS CAN BE HURTFUL AND DAMAGING IF WE LET THE FIRST THING BLURT OUT OF OUR MOUTHS. LET'S TAKE CARE, BECAUSE WHEN WE HURT OTHER PEOPLE, IT ENDS UP HURTING US TOO.

VİOLENCE İS NOT OK

It is not OK for anyone to hit, push or touch you. No one has the right to do so. If someone is hurting you, you have the right to say no and you have the right to tell someone about it, to ensure it does not happen again. Your body is sacred and special and it is yours and only yours. Say no to those who would act in violence against you and if you notice violence against someone else, tell someone you can trust, so it can stop. Violence is not OK.

Say NO to violence.

MY BODY İS SACRED. İ DECİDE WHO GOES NEAR ME.

It can be difficult not to compare
ourselves to others - But you are
your perfect You. There is no one
else exactly like you in the whole
entire world. I think that makes
you pretty special.

Our bodies continuously change our whole entire lives. What you look like today will be different to next year. Everybody changes at a different rate, no two people change at the exact same time. Be kind to your body and nurture yourself, because you are worth it.

You know how this works now - so it's your turn! It's time to put pen to paper and write your own warm fuzzy. You can write one, two or even three if you like, the important thing is that you write at least one. Pick something you like about yourself and write it on a piece of paper and stick it somewhere where you will see it every day. That could be a spot next to your bed or on a mirror, in a diary or even in your wallet. Read this warm fuzzy to yourself every single day.

Now for something a little different but equally as important. Pick something you don't like about yourself and turn it into a positive. For instance, I never use to like my hair and I don't like it when I get angry. So I wrote onto a piece of paper, "I have beautiful shinny healthy hair" and "I remain calm in every situation and I listen to what others have to say." Now it's your turn. You can write one, two or ten of them if you want to. Stick it somewhere where you will see it every day and watch how magically your thoughts can change.

IT IS OK FOR ME TO SAY NO

If I feel unsafe or if it feels wrong to me, I can and will say NO. I make sure that I am OK and if I am not, I SAY NO. It is OK for me to say NO.

WE ARE ALL BEAUTIFUL CHILDREN OF THE WORLD. WE ARE ALL THE SAME. WE LIVE DIFFERENT LIVES IN DIFFERENT COUNTRIES, FOLLOWING DIFFERENT RELIGIONS AND GOING TO DIFFERENT SCHOOLS, BUT WE ARE ALL THE SAME. LET'S TAKE CARE OF EACH OTHER SO THAT WE MAY ALL BE WELL, EAT WELL AND LIVE WELL TOGETHER.

Our minds are not the same. The experiences we have are very different from each other. For instance I do not like ice-cream as it makes me sick in the tummy (don't worry I still love chocolate). I don't like dogs because when I was younger one bit me on the leg and now I am afraid. You may love dogs and ice-cream, dancing and singing too. Each of us will have different experiences. That is why other people sometimes don't understand what we are feeling or what we are saying, simply because they have not experienced the same as us or their experience of it was very different from ours. Be patient with those who don't quite get what you are talking about, it doesn't mean they don't love you, like you or that they don't want to understand you, it's just that they don't see it the same way as you do. Be patient, listen to others and don't be afraid to let them know when you don't quite get what they are saying or feeling. Our minds are different and that is OK.

My friend told me, it doesn't matter what other people think of you, it's none of your business anyway. I like this. I like this because we will never know what is in other people's heads, ever. We will never know what they are thinking or what they are saying when we are not around... and guess what, no one will ever really know what you are thinking about. We can tell people what we are thinking, but they don't really know whether we are thinking it or not. Thinking about what other people are thinking about us and thinking if they are thinking about what we are thinking, MY GOODNESS! EXHAUSTING! The only thought that matters is what you think of you. I know how hard it is to block out what you think people think of you, but you will never truly know. Focus on the nice things you have to say about yourself and the way you see yourself. Trust me, other people can see your inner beauty. Sometimes people are afraid of it and pick on you because of it, but it doesn't mean you're ugly. You are beautiful.

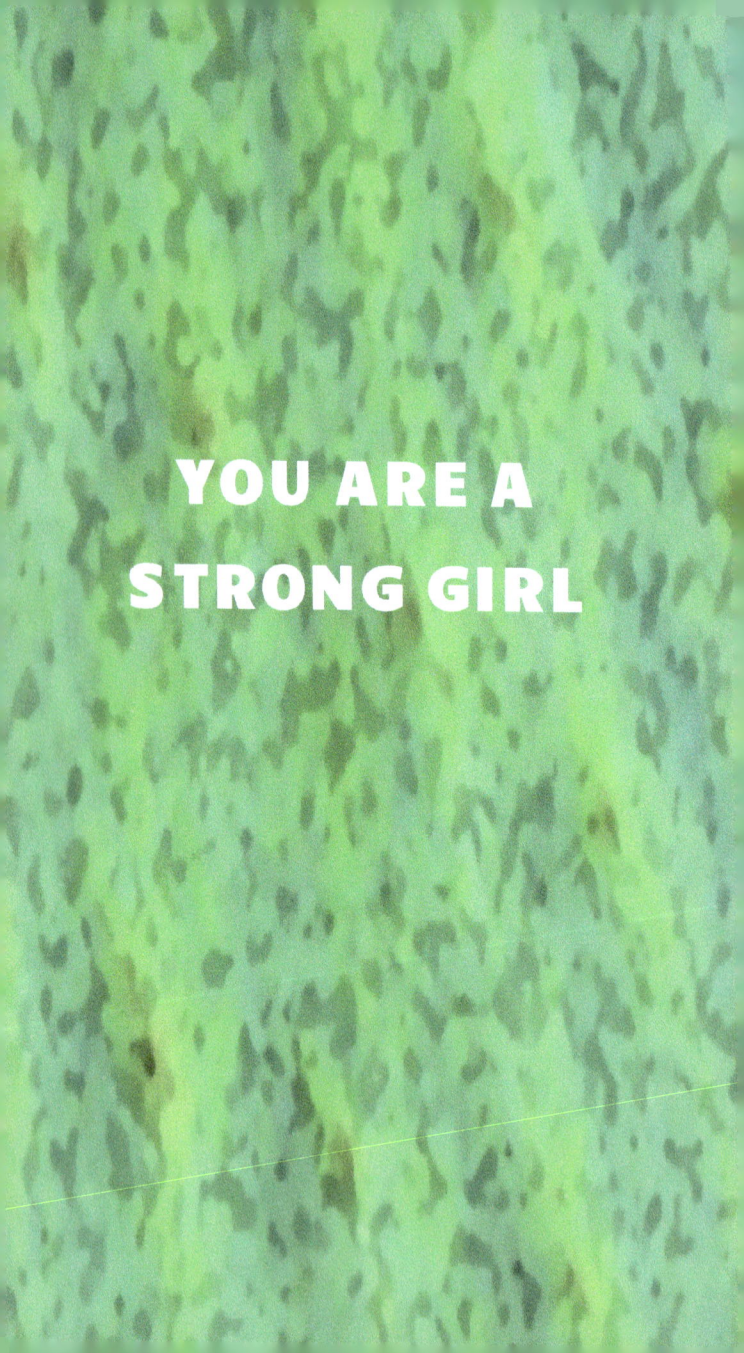

I CAN HANDLE ANY TRICKY SITUATION

You may not get it today, but it is possible you will tomorrow and if not tomorrow, maybe the day after or the day after that. Persistence is the key. Try something new or a different way, but keep going. Most importantly keep believing, because I believe in you.

People will try to tell you what the proper family is, the way to be brought up, the proper parents, the right schools, right friends, gurus and whatever else they deem necessary to get you to follow them or participate. Choose your own path. What feels right to you, is right for you.

THE BEAUTY OF LIFE IS
THERE'S SO MUCH TO
DISCOVER...

SO MANY DIFFERENCES,
SO MANY PEOPLE...

IT'S EXCITING TO
DISCOVER NEW THINGS.

I RESPECT OTHER
PEOPLE'S TRADITIONS

I RESPECT MYSELF

I RESPECT MY ENVIRONMENT

MY SKIN IS UNIQUE

TO ME AND IT IS

BEAUTIFUL

I appreciate my differences
they are a part of me!

I do my best to appreciate
other people's differences too.

When you call me nasty names it hurts... it hurts me as it would hurt you. I cry alone so that no one knows, but I feel it slowly destroying my soul.

Let's make a promise to ourselves, that we will not call others by mean names, nor shall we call ourselves by any mean name, because both of us deserve to be loved. We are beautiful and special in our own different ways.

IT FEELS SO GOOD TO SMILE

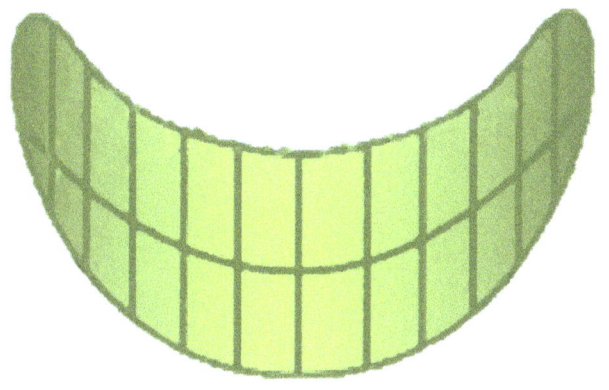

CHOOSE 3 PEOPLE TO SMILE AT TODAY.
EVEN IF THEY DON'T SMILE BACK, I BET
IT MADE THEM FEEL REAL GOOD INSIDE.

YOU HAVE BEAUTIFUL HAIR!

YOU HAVE SPARKLEY EYES TOO!

Sometimes life can be confusing and feel pretty hard at times. When you feel this way come back to simplicity. Simply ask yourself, what is it that I want to achieve? Go back to basics. Is there another way this can be done? Stop and check in with your feelings, be honest with yourself. You are your greatest friend and you will always support yourself, no matter the outcome.

YOU CAN BE whatever you want to BE. Some people may say that it is impossible or that you're not good enough, but don't believe a word they say, YOU CAN DO IT. Choose what you want to be, then make a step-by-step plan and be willing to put in the work to get there AND above all BELIEVE, because YOU CAN BE whatever it is you want to be.

BEING SILLY IS FUN!!

WHETHER IT'S DRESSING UP DANCING AROUND OR TELLING A JOKE - HAVE SOME FUN TODAY.

I AM FUN!

What can you do today to make someone smile?

I CONTINUE TO GROW INTO A

MORE AMAZING PERSON EVERY DAY

I CHOOSE TO SURROUND MYSELF WITH

AMAZING PEOPLE WHO SUPPORT ME

FEELING PEACE INSIDE

WHEN LIFE FEELS A LITTLE CRAZY, TRY SITTING ON YOUR OWN IN A QUIET ROOM. CLOSE YOUR EYES AND FOCUS ON YOUR BREATH. COUNT YOUR BREATH SLOWLY IN AND OUT. START BY COUNTING TO 30 AND MAKE YOUR WAY TO 90 AND THEN BEYOND. SEE IF THAT MAKES YOU FEEL MORE PEACEFUL INSIDE. IT WORKS FOR ME ON MY MOST CRAZIEST OF DAYS.

I AM UNDERSTANDING
I AM INTELLIGENT
I AM TALENTED
I AM CARING
I AM FUN
I AM AMAZING
I AM FABULOUS
I AM EXTRAORDINARY
I AM FANTASTIC
I AM BRILLIANT
I AM SUPER
I AM ME
I LIKE ME

The more you say it, the more you believe it. So if you don't believe it, I think you should say it at least 20 times today. You are all these things and MORE.

I WALK TALL AND PROUD

Squeeze your shoulder bones together in the center of your back. Tighten and tense your stomach muscles. Now walk and repeat:

I WALK TALL AND PROUD

If I feel nervous before walking into a room, I always use this trick. It always makes me feel better and more confident.

THE BUTTERFLY

So beautiful and free. Gliding through the air, peaceful and purposeful. Before the butterfly can become so free, it has to go through a transition. The start of its life begins as a little caterpillar, learning and growing, just as we are. We start off little and begin to grow, spreading our wings as we go. Our transition is not always easy and it can be quite tough, but have patience with yourself, because you are becoming that beautiful butterfly.

I AM BEAUTIFUL & FREE

Sometimes my life seems like a giant web. I created that web and I know how to break through it. I trust myself to know exactly what to do.

Sometimes I'm a busy little bee.

Today I stop and take some time especially for me.

YOU ARE A GOOD PERSON

I AM DEVELOPING EVERY DAY
Some days I know exactly what I am doing and other days I have no idea...
and that is OK.

I HELP OTHERS SEE HOW EXTRAORDINARY THEY ARE TOO

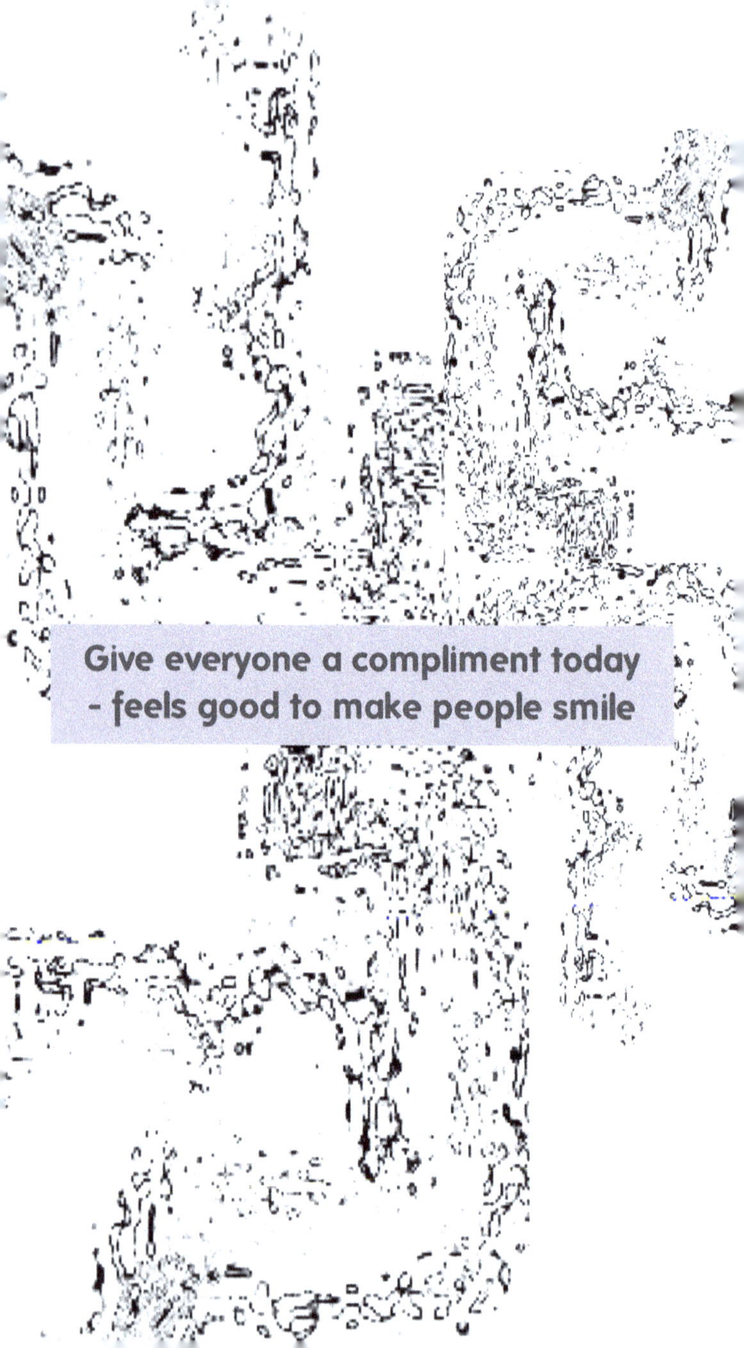

Give everyone a compliment today - feels good to make people smile

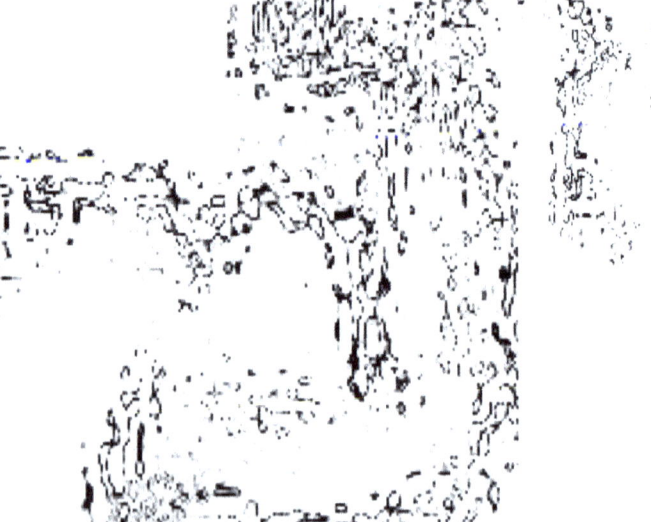

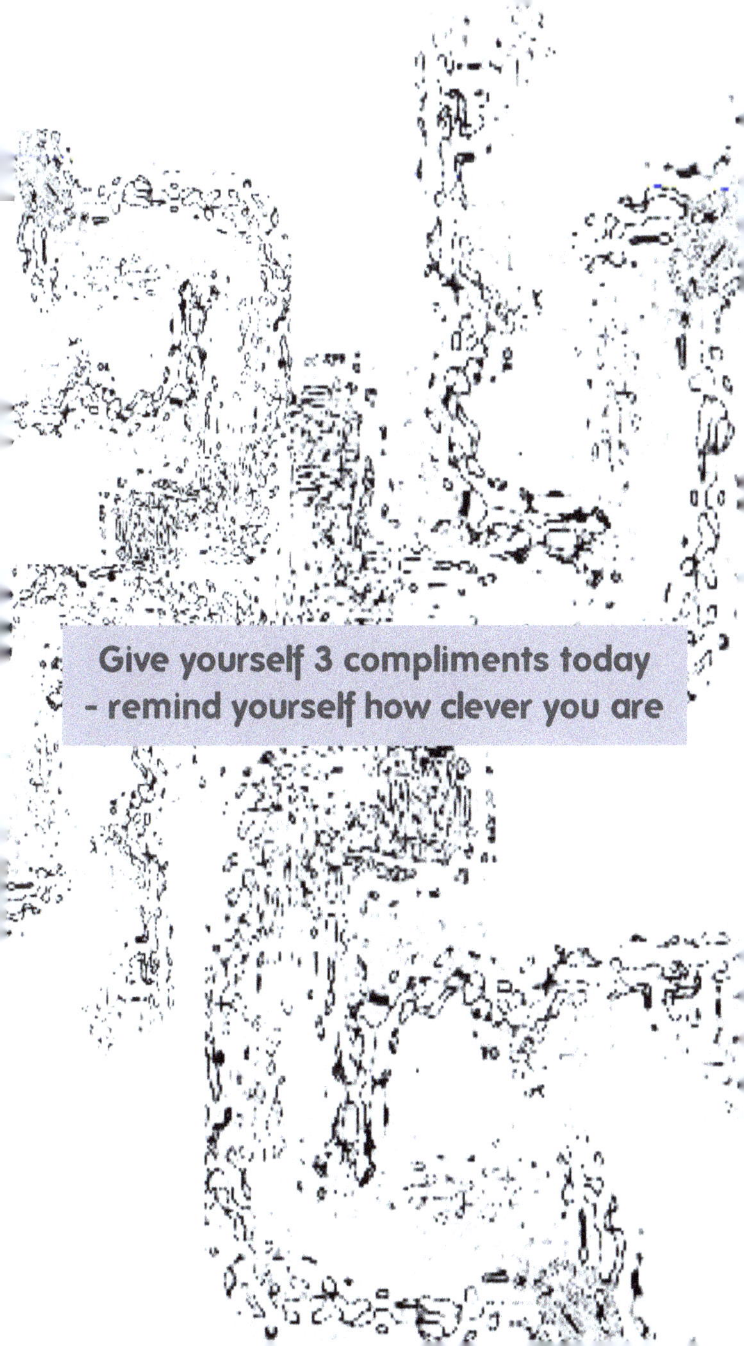

Give yourself 3 compliments today - remind yourself how clever you are

BE YOUR FAVOURITE YOU

FAVORITE THINGS… some of my favorite things are dancing, swimming, riding motorbikes, playing monopoly, watching soccer, SHOES!!! They can be high heels, boots, sneakers, flip flops… you name it, I like it! Our favorite things don't have to be the same, they can be girly and boyish or whatever you like. They are YOUR favorite things. Enjoy one of your favorite things today.

I CHOOSE TODAY TO GIVE MYSELF THE BEST LIFE EVER

Sometimes we need to BEE flexible

BEE flexible today

BEE Willing to SEE it from another point of view ... ALL our views ARE important

A feeling is just a feeling. It cannot physically harm me. It is safe for me to feel sad and cry when I need to. Once I have felt the feeling, I can let it go and begin to feel better. Sometimes it takes more time than I originally thought, but I will eventually begin to feel better.

İ KNOW THE THİNGS İ KNOW

İ TRUST MY İNNER GUİDE

İ LİSTEN TO THAT FEELİNG İNSİDE

FEELING scared is a warning sign that something is not right. Assess the danger before deciding on your next move. You can detect when it is genuine fear for your safety and if you feel unsafe, then act accordingly and remove yourself from the situation.

WHEN I am scared to take the next step forward because of fear of getting up on stage, talking in front of the class, submitting a piece of work or even making new friends - I TAKE a DEEP BREATH IN and I take that step forward anyway. For I know that each new thing I do, I become stronger and better, building my skills. If it doesn't work out today, there is always tomorrow, next week, next month... hey! EVEN Next Year. It will all be OK... because fear of performing a task such as public speaking can be overcome and is different to having fear for my safety.

It's challenging when I don't understand other people's point of view.

However, everybody else's experience of the world is different to mine.

It is OK for me to see the world as I do and I allow others to see it their way too.

Not everything is Black or White.

Nor is some things Wrong or Right.

Sometimes things aren't what they seem to be, so I have to trust how it feels to me.

I NO LONGER ALLOW
FEAR TO STOP ME FROM
ACHIEVING MY GOALS

I TAKE A STEP FORWARD

I NO LONGER DOUBT
MY ABILITIES TO
ACHIEVE MY GOALS

I AM EXTRAORDINARY

I'M NOT AFRAID TO ASK FOR HELP

IT IS A SIGN OF COURAGE

NOT WEAKNESS

BEE WHAT IS

VISUALIZE how you want to be.

Close your eyes and see yourself in your greatest light, being all that you want to be. Then open your eyes and BE WHAT IS.

Be, Act, Live, exactly what you imagined.

BEE WHAT IS

I LET GO

I CAN LET GO OF ALL THE THINGS
THAT MAKE ME FEEL BAD.

I CHOOSE TO LET THEM GO

I AM LETTING GO

Has someone upset you and you are feeling angry with how you were treated? Hold an image of that person in your mind and ask yourself, is there something missing here? Is that person sad or down? Maybe they are hurting too? It's not OK for someone to be mean to you, but we can still wish them well. Let's put the image of that person in a boat and push it out to sea, wishing them love and peace as you let them go. The longer they linger in your mind, the longer they can continue to hurt you. We can choose to Let them Go.

*My Heart is Open
I am Extremely
Loveable*

I Can Be My Loveable Self

I AM CAPABLE

I ACHIEVE ALL THAT I WANT TO ACHIEVE

I LEARN FROM MY PAST
MISTAKES

THEY TEACH ME HOW TO
DO THINGS BETTER

I KNOW WHO I AM

Write a description of who you are. Describe yourself in the most positive words you can think of. When you feel a little low, pull this description out and read how fabulous you are.

I KNOW WHERE I AM GOING

Write a description of everything you want to be, where you are going and what it looks like. Try reading this every morning and see how good it makes you feel. It will keep you focused too.

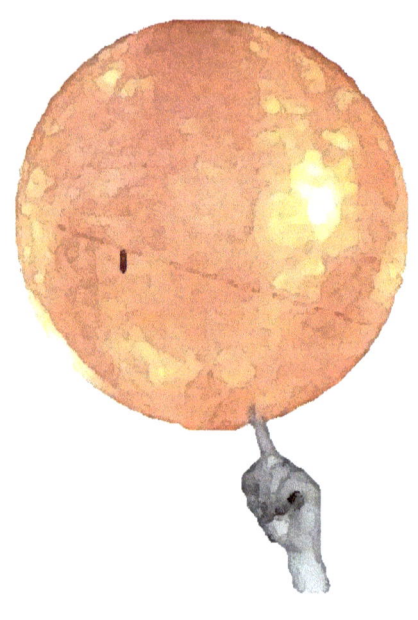

İ LOVE ME TO THE MOON AND BACK

MY MIND IS CLEAR

I AM MAKING THE RIGHT CHOICES FOR ME

LOVE CAN GO FOREVER
It will never run out and
there is plenty of it for all of us.
Never be afraid to lose it as
there will always be more.

Pick 3 people that you struggle to be nice to. Now pick one good thing about each of them. Next time they cross your path, focus on the good thing you picked. Sending good vibes to others, is like sending good vibes to ourselves. It feels nice to be nice, even if someone else is mean. It's all about how we feel inside.

I am not defined by where I come from, what school I went to nor what my parents do. What defines me is who I am and what I want to do.

I am only limited by my own thoughts, therefore I choose today to have no limitations on me. If I can think it, I can do it.

İ allow My CREATİVİTY to flow without inhibition nor QUESTİON. İ Pray that LOVİNG People Surround & SUPPORT Me and that İ ALWAYS have the Tools to follow through and COMPLETE the task with LOVE in My HEART.

I am capable of achieving
anything & everything!

I hold the remote control
to my life.

YOU ARE STRONG

The strength will be there when you need it and you will gain strength from those around you. There is always support for you.

I AM STRONG
I AM SUPPORTED
I SUPPORT ME

Every day is a new day, a chance to start fresh. What do YOU want to do today? What do YOU want to show the world today? As you splash your face with water, imagine yesterday going down the drain and start today with new possibilities.

I AM KIND TO ME TODAY

IF YOU CANNOT SEE THE ROAD AHEAD AND YOU DON'T KNOW WHICH DIRECTION TO TAKE, TRY A ROAD MAP. WRITE DOWN YOUR GOAL IN THE MIDDLE OF A PIECE OF PAPER, THEN DRAW LOTS OF LINES FROM THE CENTRE OF YOUR GOAL -AND AT THE END OF THOSE LINES, WRITE ALL THE OPTIONS YOU CAN THINK OF, ON HOW YOU CAN ACHIEVE YOUR GOAL. MAPS CAN HELP US GET CLEAR.

WHEN I COME TO A DEAD-END, I FIND A NEW DIRECTION TO TAKE. THERE ARE ENDLESS OPTIONS FOR ME.

TRUST THAT YOU WILL KNOW
WHICH DIRECTION TO TAKE

Sometimes it gets confusing, so try being quiet, block out all the noise and listen to that voice within. It will help you to know which way to go.

THERE ARE NO LIMITATIONS

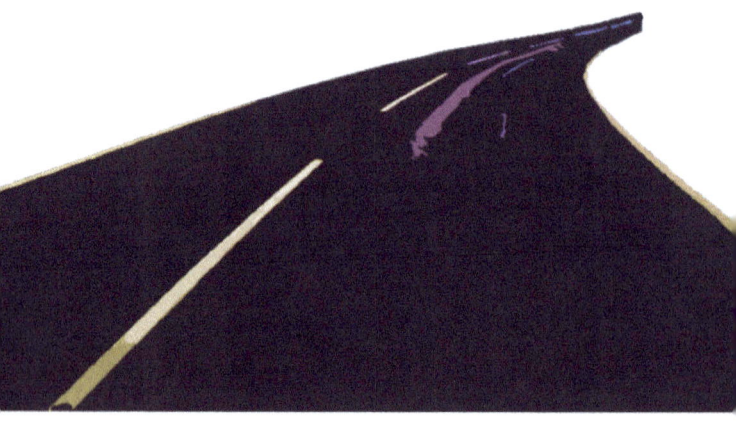

THE ROAD IS ENDLESS with endless possibilities. Your imagination has no limitation. Start imagining today how your life can be, follow your own path, to a destination that you choose.

I AM LIMITLESS AND FREE

If I say I can't do, then I can't do it. If I say I can do it, then I CAN DO IT! Believe in yourself today and feel the freedom when you believe you can achieve anything.

YOU CAN GO ANYWHERE IN THE WORLD

YOU CAN BE ANYTHING YOU WANT TO BE!

I'M SITTING ON TOP OF THE WORLD

AND I FEEL GREAT

Sometimes it seems like everyone has it all together, that they aren't worried about anything, that they feel fabulous and great all the time and that they know exactly where they are going. Let me tell you, this is not the case. The truth is, we are all a little worried from time to time. We sometimes think we are too fat, too thin, too short, too tall, too white, too brown, too loud, too quiet, not smart enough, not sure if I'll make it, break it, take it, you name it, we're all feeling a little unsure. No matter how old or young we are, we question. Even the most "together" people have their ups and downs, their days of doubt and giving up. The trick is to accept it when you feel that way and know that it shall pass. For you have endless possibilities and are perfect just as you are.

I ACCEPT THE WAY

I FEEL TODAY

I take care of MY body
I take care of MY mind

Just as filling your body with fresh fruits and vegetables fills you with nutrients that help you to shine, so does the positive, loving, nurturing thoughts you have about yourself. You radiate a unique inner beauty. Make sure you keep reminding yourself of how beautiful you are.

MY BODY IS BEAUTIFUL

BELIEVE IN YOURSELF

BELIEVE IN YOUR ABILITIES

When a negative thought enters your mind and you begin to say, "I'm stupid, I'm silly." HALT IT and repeat to yourself,

I BELIEVE IN ME

If you can find a mirror, look at yourself and repeat it 3 times.

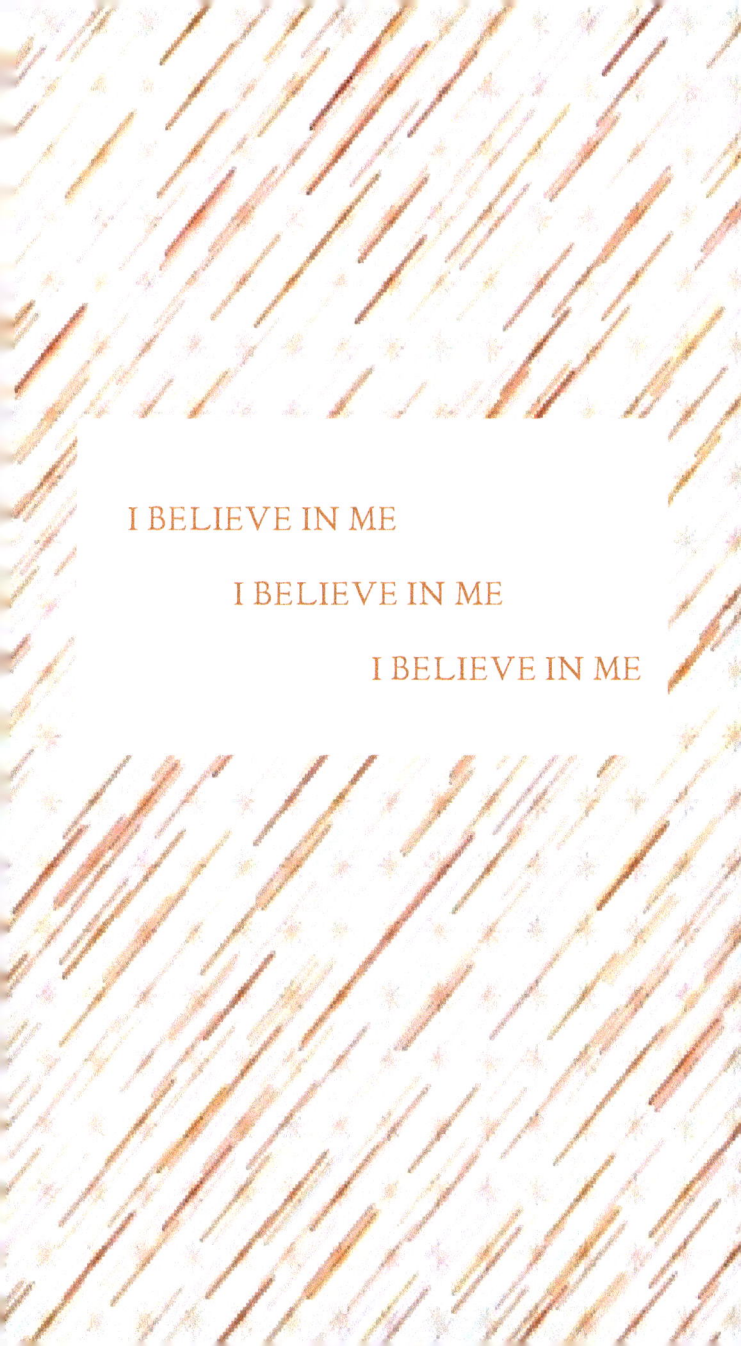

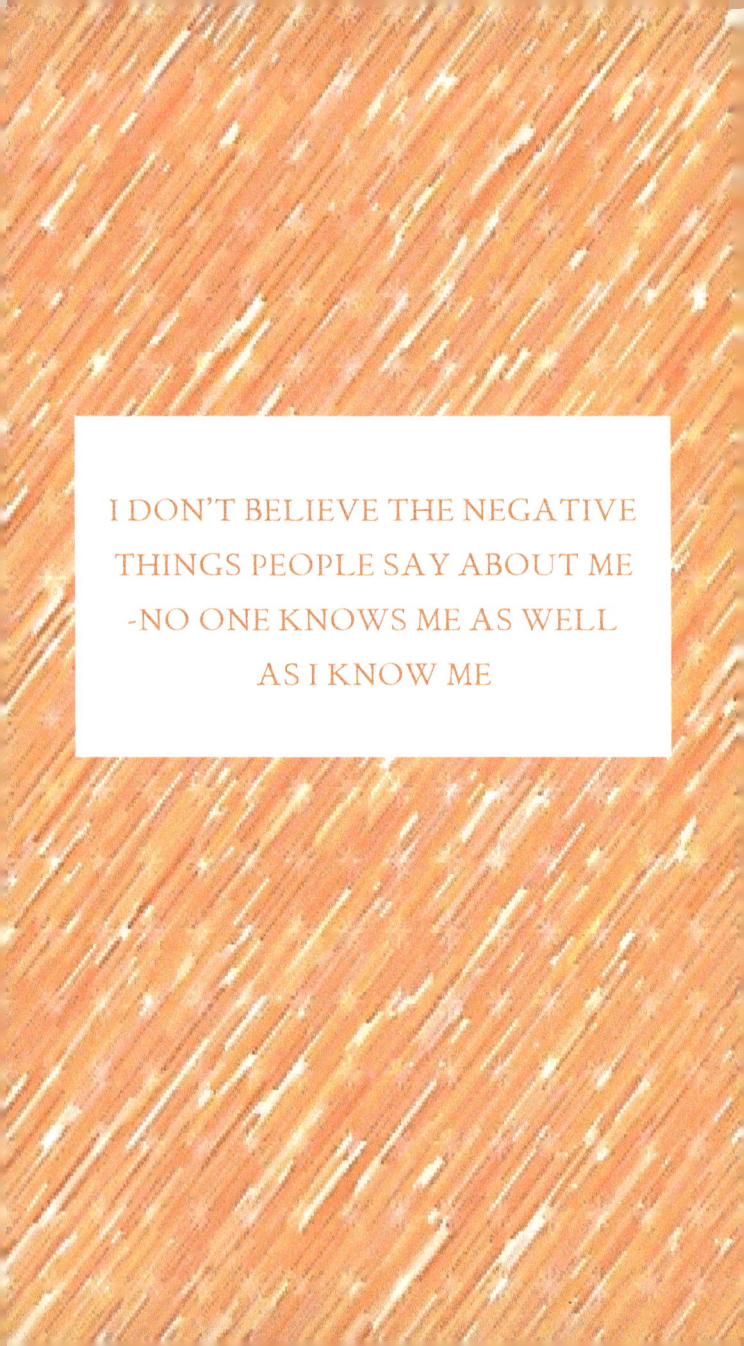

When people call me stupid or an idiot, it can make me angry and sometimes it can hurt. They don't know what they are talking about. I am smart and funny and learning the way that I learn. I am not the same as everybody else and that is what makes me special. I am different to you and I am different to everyone else. That is what makes us all special -we are different to each other.

Find a Mirror and sit in front of it

Look yourself in the eye and count to 30

Can you see it? The sparkle?

That special light inside your eyes?

Your eyes shine brightly, twinkling all

of your possibilities.

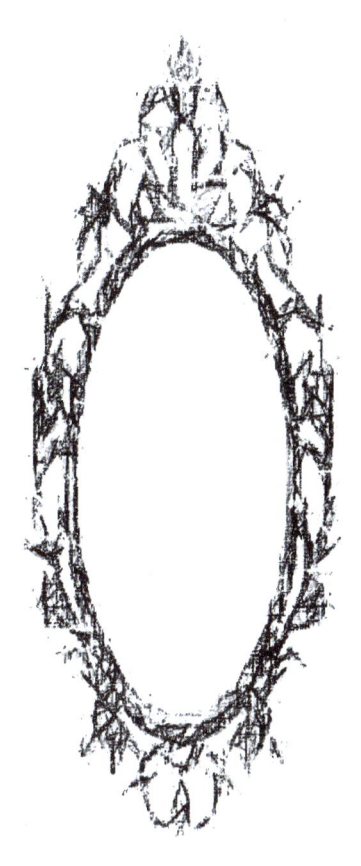

The Mirror is my friend...

I can see how Beautiful I AM

WHAT QUALITIES DO YOU LIKE ABOUT YOURSELF?

WHAT WOULD YOU LIKE
TO IMPROVE?

ARE THERE LITTLE STEPS
THAT YOU CAN TAKE TO
GET YOU THERE?

Can you treat yourself with a special experience today? Maybe you could paint your toes, eat your favorite food or simply dance to your favorite song. Do something that makes you feel Special.

You Are Special

Close your eyes and imagine yourself at your very best. See yourself surrounded by amazing people and great friends. Does it make you smile? It makes me smile.

TODAY I BELIEVE I CAN ACHIEVE AMAZING THINGS

TODAY
I KNOW
THAT I AM
SPECIAL

Shoot for the stars...

No dream is too big when you take it one step at a time.

When I look up into the night sky and see thousands of stars, I know there is always hope. This moment, as all moments, will pass. There will always be new opportunities, new people, new places, in which I will go, meet and have. So look up into the night sky and make a wish, knowing that anything is possible for tomorrow.

I AM

A STAR

I CAN

DO IT

Every time you say I can't, repeat 3 times:
I CAN I CAN I CAN
Now let's try again

MAKE 3 WISHES
What are 3 things you can do this week to help them come true?

No one else is in charge of your mind... so DREAM. DREAM BIG.

As far and wide as your imagination can cross, to the bottomless ocean and endless sky, there are no limitations... they are your Dreams.

DREAM FAR & WIDE.

I follow my Dreams

I can be, do and have ALL that I desire.

FRIENDSHIP

Is not about wanting to change someone to fit your life. It's about accepting them exactly as they are, being there when they need you most AND never saying, "I told you so." You must respect each other, listen to each other and say kind things to one another. A friend will never make you feel bad about who you are, just as you will never make her feel bad for who she is. Real friendship feels peaceful.

LOVE

Love, oh love! The stuff that makes you go crazy at times and act real silly too. It's OK, we ALL do it... but with true love, you never have to change. You are enough. You are You. True love does not stifle you, it does not stop you from growing, from living your dreams and being who you truly are. True love does not hurt you nor does it ever put you down. True love feels good.

I AM WORTH LISTENING TO

I know people are busy and sometimes I may not pick the right moment to talk about something that is important to me, but what I do know is that I am worth listening to. What I have to say is important. I am important and I deserve to be heard.

I AM LISTENING
    I PAY ATTENTION

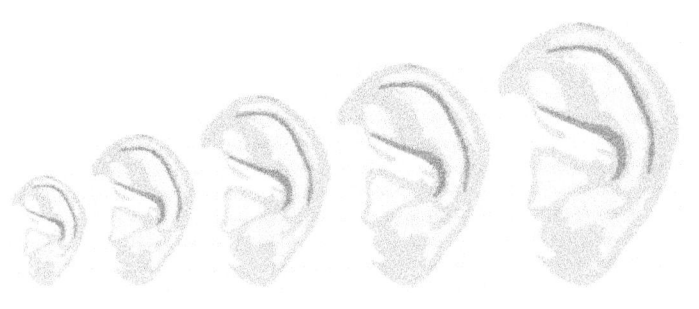

I LISTEN TO WHAT OTHERS HAVE TO SAY

fghdsjfghkhsdjhfjdksghdsjhgds
bhcbsdhjkfgauriebgfhjbsajdhbf
hgjryotyuieoyrhgjldfbjvhbdfjhvh
kjhehgvuwirytuiguyeriyietrghjfk

SomeTimES EVerYthiNG FeELs LikE MUmbo JUmbo AnD I cAN't qUIte WOrk ouT WhaT tO Do.

IT IS GOING TO BE OK.
You may not know today but
you might know tomorrow.
Let it Go and Trust You
Will work it out.

When I'm confused and I'm not sure what to do, I sit down on my own and I write out my problems onto a piece of paper. I then write down the best outcome that I can see. I read over my problem and the best outcome, then I take a deep breath and throw the paper in the bin. It feels good not to worry about it, I can now let it go. I've thrown the piece of paper away. I don't have to carry the worry with me anymore. I'll know what to do.

YOU ARE
ALLOWED TO ASK
QUESTIONS
IT IS SMART TO
DO SO

**YOU ARE
INTELLIGENT**

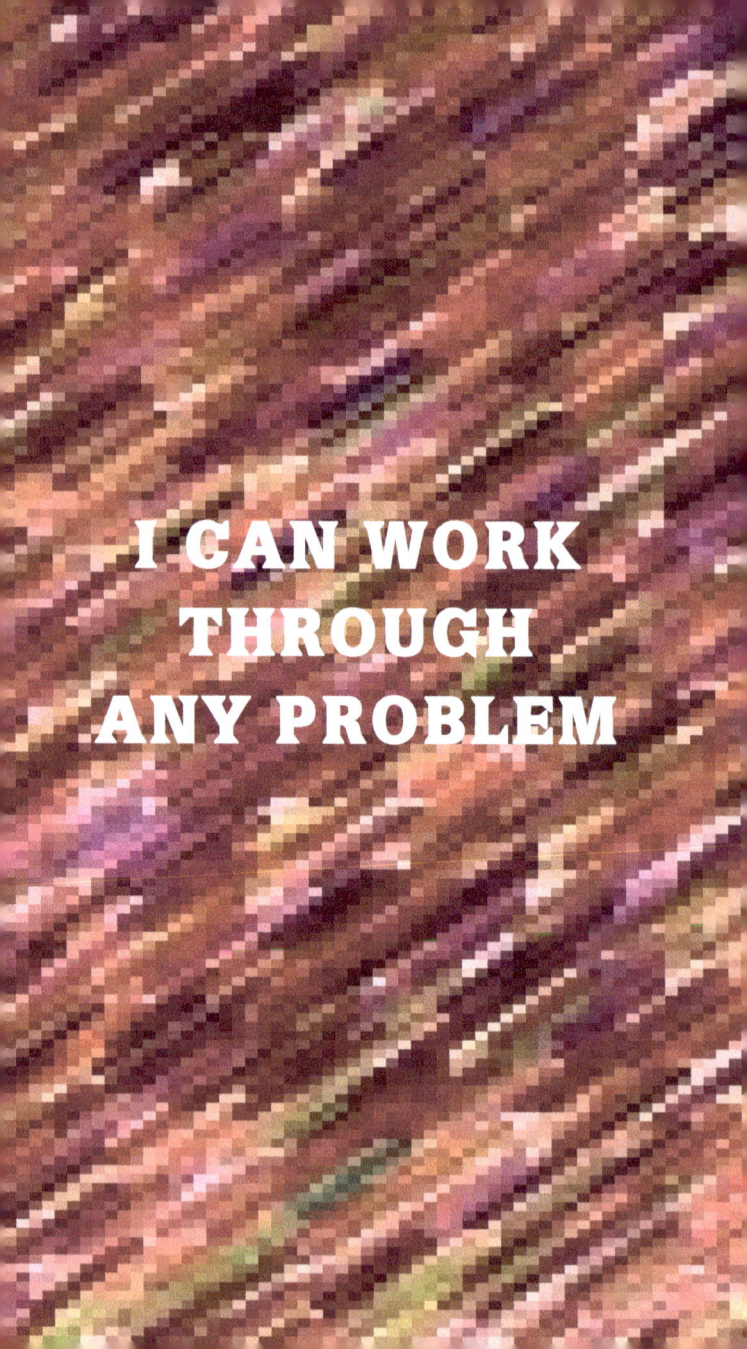

I CAN FIND THE ANSWER

IT'S TIME TO SMILE

LIST 3 THINGS YOU ARE GRATEFUL FOR TODAY:

1

2

3

RECOGNIZE YOUR TALENTS

LIST 3 THINGS YOU ARE REALLY GOOD AT:

1

2

3

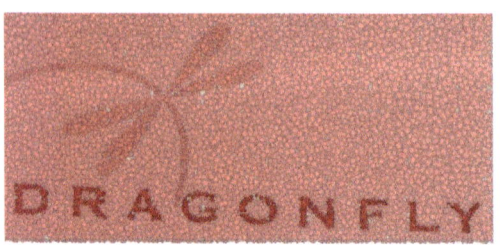

The Dragonfly, much like the butterfly, represents change. This beautiful creature journeys through a deep transformation before taking flight. Like the Dragonfly, you will also undertake a huge transformation. You will emerge strong, graceful, beautiful. Stay true to who you are and nurture yourself along the way. YOUR best friend is YOU. Kind words must start with you. Your beauty is in a cocoon, building, ready to flourish. Share your beauty with those who nurture you, those who respect you, those who see you for the magnificent dragonfly within.

*I HAVE THE
FREEDOM
TO BE
ME
& I LIKE IT!*

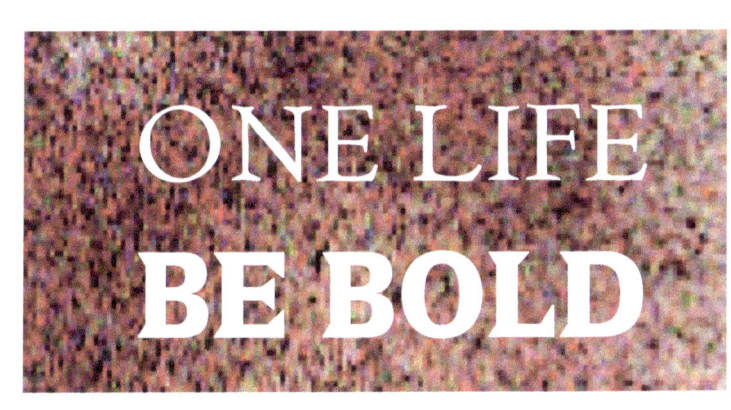

I want you to take a colored pen and mark on the map where you are in the world. Make it a very small little dot. It's almost as though you cannot see the dot at all. I want you to imagine how many other little dots there are out there in the world. There are so many little dots, that it would be impossible to fit them all on this map. Sometimes it seems so important what the girl we sit next to in class thinks of us and the people in the playground, the ones we play sport against and the ones we hang out with at lunch, as well as the people we want to be liked by. It seems as though it matters exactly what each of these people thinks of us. If our clothes look OK, if we have the right hair, if we can play sport, sing the song in tune or even if we have painted our nails the right color. It seems as though it matters so much of what each person thinks of us that we forget what we think of ourselves. Not everyone is going to like the top we choose to wear, or what we had for lunch, how we walk or even how we talk. We aren't here to please every person. We are here to enjoy our lives. Not everyone in the world has the right pair of shoes or even a pair of shoes at all! So if today we get picked on or looked upon with disgust or spat at with cruel words, just remember they are only one of billions of little colored dots and what they say is so incredibly small against the whole entire world. There are many other people who have the same as me, less than me and more than me. It does not matter what they think of me nor what they say of me, because I matter to me.

This is so important that I think it's best we read this today and tomorrow, remembering that not only are we one tiny dot in the world, but so is everybody else.

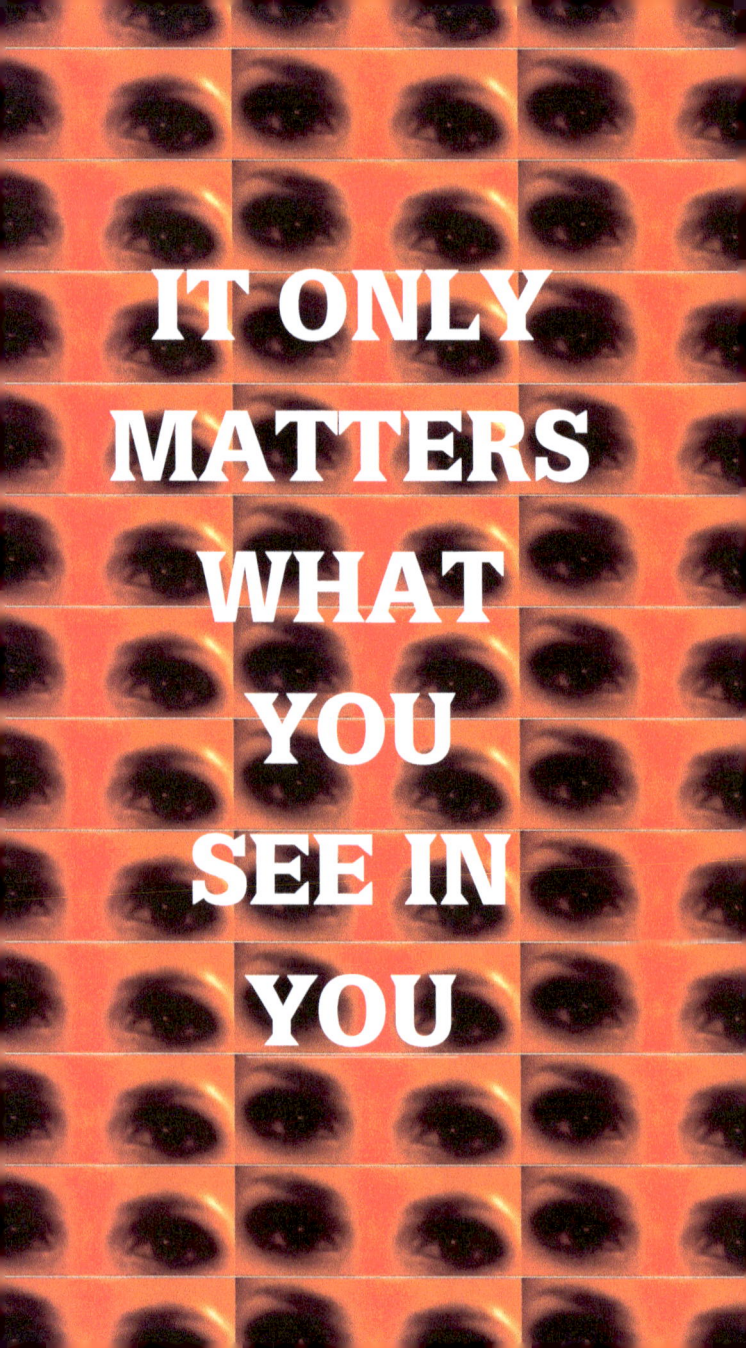

You are constantly changing. The great thing about life is you choose every day who you are and what you want to be. Change is good... and you get to choose the change within you.

I AM HERE

I SEE ME
I SEE WHAT I NEED
I SEE HOW TO ASK

I SEE HOW I FEEL
I SEE HOW OTHERS FEEL
I SEE WHAT OTHERS NEED

I SEE ME
I SEE YOU

I SEE WE CAN WORK TOGETHER

YOU ME WE

**OTHERS
ME AND YOU**

When others don't want to work together, it's OK. I can offer for us all to work together, but ultimately it's everybody's individual choice. I will keep the invitation open, but I give everyone his or her space. Perhaps later everyone will see that it's far easier for us all if we work together. Two heads really are better than one, if we choose to work together.

YOU ME WE

DANCE

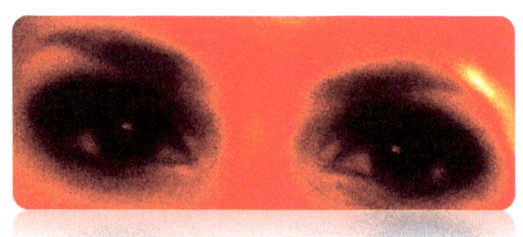

LIKE NO ONE IS WATCHING

Play your favorite song, grab your hairbrush & sing like you've never sung before! Have fun

I AM LIMITLESS

I no longer blame others… really, the
only person that can limit me is me!

Now that feels good to know…
I am moving forward knowing that
I can be whatever I want to be.

There are no limits to my abilities
and what I can achieve.
I am limitless…
I am ME!

The Only Limitations are My Imagination

GO TO THE MIRROR AND SAY TO YOURSELF "I LOVE YOU"

AND SMILE - IT FEELS SILLY - BUT THE MORE YOU

SAY IT - THE MORE IT STARTS TO FEEL REALLY GOOD!

TRY AND SAY IT EVERY DAY THIS WEEK

I ♥ TO Smile

paris

I ♥ TO Laugh

paris

I LAUGH AND SMILE ALL THE TIME AND I'M ALLOWED TO BE HAPPY.

Thank you Mary Craven

& Class of 1992 - 7 Green

& Class of 1997 - 12 Red

www.ingramcontent.com/pod-product-compliance
Lightning Source LLC
Chambersburg PA
CBHW040327300426
44113CB00020B/2674